CORE LANGUAGE SKILLS

Rhymes and Rhythms

Kara Murray

PowerKiDS press™

New York

Published in 2015 by The Rosen Publishing Group, Inc.
29 East 21st Street, New York, NY 10010

First Edition

Editor: Sarah Machajewski
Book Design: Reann Nye

Photo Credits: Cover Christopher Futcher/Vetta/Getty Images; p. 5 Darrin Henry/Shutterstock.com; p. 9 (dog) Inna Astakhova/Shutterstock.com; p. 9 (frog) kazoka/Shutterstock.com; p. 9 (log) josefauer/Shutterstock.com; p. 9 (hog) panbazil/Shutterstock.com; pp. 11, 17 (pencil) Julia Ivantsova/Shutterstock.com; p. 12 Traveller Martin/Shutterstock.com; p. 15 Sergey Novikov/Shutterstock.com; p.18 Cavan Images/Digital Vision/Getty Images; p. 19 (boy) Valeriy Lebedev/Shutterstock.com; p. 19 (girl) Serhiy Kobyakov/Shutterstock.com; p. 21 2A Images/Getty Images.

Library of Congress Cataloging-in-Publication Data

Murray, Kara.
Rhymes and rhythms / by Kara Murray.
p. cm. — (Core language skills)
Includes index.
ISBN 978-1-4777-7369-7 (pbk.)
ISBN 978-1-4777-7370-3 (6-pack)
ISBN 978-1-4777-7368-0 (library binding)
1. English language — Rhyme — Juvenile literature. 2. English language — Rhythm — Juvenile literature. 3. English language — Versification — Juvenile literature. 4. Literary form — Juvenile literature. 5. Poetics — Juvenile literature. I. Murray, Kara. II. Title
PE1505.M87 2015
821.009—d23

Manufactured in the United States of America

CPSIA Compliance Information: Batch #CW15PK: For Further Information contact Rosen Publishing, New York, New York at 1-800-237-9932

CONTENTS

RHYME TIME

Read the following sentence out loud: "It's time to learn how to rhyme!" You may notice that "rhyme" and "time" sound alike. That's what a rhyme is—two words that sound the same.

Rhyming words have the same ending sounds. They may start with different letters, or they may be spelled differently. That's okay! As long as the ending sounds match, the words rhyme.

Rhyming helps us learn all the different sounds words can make. This helps us speak, read, and write better. Rhyming can be fun. Read on to see what you can do with rhyming words.

Figure It Out

What is a rhyme?

Find the answer to this question and the others in this book on page 22.

Rhyming is all about the way words sound, whether you say them out loud or write them down.

ALL IN THE FAMILY

The first step in learning how to rhyme is to become familiar with different sounds. Every word in the English language sounds a certain way. Where does the sound come from? It comes from the letters that make up the word.

Each letter has its own sound. When you put letters together, you **combine** their sounds and make a word. Groups of words that have the same letters and the same sound are called word families. The shared letters and sound are found at the end of all the words in the family.

Figure It Out

The word family "-at" has many members. "Fat" and "hat" are two examples. Can you think of more words that belong to the "-at" family?

Word Families

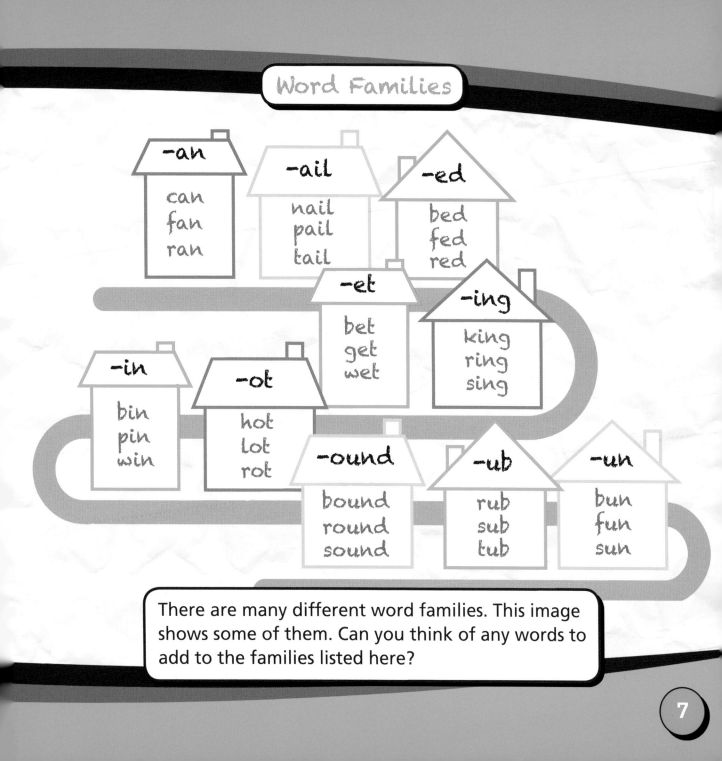

-an
can
fan
ran

-ail
nail
pail
tail

-ed
bed
fed
red

-et
bet
get
wet

-ing
king
ring
sing

-in
bin
pin
win

-ot
hot
lot
rot

-ound
bound
round
sound

-ub
rub
sub
tub

-un
bun
fun
sun

There are many different word families. This image shows some of them. Can you think of any words to add to the families listed here?

TELLING SPELLING

Let's try using word families to help us rhyme. Suppose you want to find words that rhyme with "dog." Break the word into its sounds. "Dog" has two—the "d" sound and the "-og" sound. The letters "-og" are a word family. Now think of other words that end in the "-og" sound. "Frog," "log," and "hog" are just a few.

The words we came up with are spelled the same except for the beginning. This can be a good trick for rhyming. If you see the same combination of letters at the end of words, they probably rhyme.

Figure It Out

Which words rhyme in the following sentences? How do you know? "Humpty Dumpty sat on a wall. Humpty Dumpty had a great fall."

dog

hog

frog

log

Spelling is one tool you can use to tell if words rhyme.
Many rhyming words share the same letters.

SOUNDS ABOUT RIGHT!

Spelling can often help you rhyme. Sometimes, however, you can throw everything you know about spelling right out the window! That's because rhyming is about the way words *sound*, not the way they're spelled. The English language has many words that rhyme even though they look nothing alike.

Why does this happen? It all goes back to the letters and the sounds they make. For example, the words "fair" and "there" are made of different letters. They rhyme because the sound made by the letters "-air" matches the sound made by the letters "-ere."

Figure It Out

The words "run," "son," and "done" rhyme, but they're all spelled differently. What makes them rhyme?

What's That Sound?

the "ate" sound	the "uhm" sound
bait	come
eight	dumb
plate	hum

the "oh" sound	the "air" sound
go	hair
sew	share
toe	wear

The words in each of these groups rhyme even though they're spelled differently. Say them out loud as you read to hear the rhyme.

POEMS FOR CHILDREN

Now that you know how to rhyme, when and where can you use it? Rhymes are used most often in **poetry**. Poems can be as short as two lines or as long as you want. Poems often have lines that end in rhyming words. Words in the same line can rhyme, too!

Nursery rhymes are poems for kids. One of the most famous is "Hey, Diddle, Diddle." This poem is shown on the next page. Can you find all the rhymes?

Figure It Out

Fill in the missing word from the following nursery rhyme. "Twinkle, twinkle, little star, How I wonder what you ___."

Hey, Diddle, Diddle

Hey, diddle, diddle,
The cat and the fiddle,
The cow jumped over the moon;
The little dog laughed
To see such sport,
And the dish ran away
with the spoon.

The rhymes in this poem are shown in different colors.
Words of the same color are words that rhyme.

GET RHYTHM

If you really love rhyming and want to use it to create your own poems, there's nothing stopping you! But there's another part of language you should know about first. It's called rhythm (RIH-thum).

Rhythm is the way the words flow in a sentence. The flow of the words creates a pattern of sounds. Patterns make things sound pleasing to our ears. Rhythm can be tough to understand because you can't see it with your eyes. You can only hear it with your ears. Let's learn how words can be used to create rhythm.

Figure It Out

What is rhythm?

Rhythm helps make poems fun to say and easy to remember.

15

STRESSED AND UNSTRESSED

In music, rhythm is the way notes flow in a song. This flow is made up of a pattern of beats. Some beats are **stressed**, or stronger. Other beats are unstressed, or weaker. Together, these beats create rhythm.

Words have stressed and unstressed parts, too. The stressed and unstressed parts are **determined** by how many **syllables** a word has. One-syllable words can be stressed or unstressed when they're used in poems. Words with many syllables have one syllable that's stronger than the others.

Figure It Out

Say the word "principal" out loud. It has three syllables. Which syllable is stressed, and which are unstressed?

Stressed or Unstressed?

Look at the following words. They're broken down into syllables and spelled in the way you **pronounce** them. The stressed part is capitalized. The unstressed part is in lowercase letters.

apple ⟶ AA-puhl
baby ⟶ BAY-bee
cat ⟶ KAT
elephant ⟶ EH-luh-fuhnt
important ⟶ ihm-POHR-tuhnt
school ⟶ SKOOL
teacher ⟶ TEE-chur

The easiest way to tell which part of a word is stressed and which part is unstressed is to say the word out loud. The strongest part is where the stress is.

Stressed and unstressed syllables affect how we pronounce a word. What happens when you put words together and create a sentence? The sentence has stressed and unstressed parts, too! Going back and forth between stressed and unstressed syllables creates rhythm, which sounds pleasing to our ears.

Figure It Out

Rewrite the following sentences to show what's stressed and what's unstressed. Say them out loud if you need help getting started. "I love to go to school. My favorite class is science."

Read the following sentences out loud: "My brother ate a sandwich. My sister ate some grapes." Do you notice a pattern? Every other syllable is stressed. You can rewrite the sentences to show what's stressed and unstressed: "my BRO-ther ATE a SAND-wich. my SIS-ter ATE some GRAPES."

Rhythm makes it fun to talk about something as simple as what you had for lunch.

Rhythm and rhyme are used all the time. It may surprise you where they pop up. We know rhythm and rhyme are important parts of poetry, but did you know they're used in music, too? Your favorite songs probably have **lyrics** that rhyme. The instruments and the way a singer sings create rhythm. For these reasons, many people think songs are "poetry set to music."

Now it's your turn to put your skills to work. Get started by thinking of words that sound the same. You may be surprised at how many words our language contains!

Figure It Out

Can you come up with words that rhyme with the words "mouse," "gate," "boat," and "ran"? Try putting some of them together to create a sentence that has rhythm.

Singing songs is great rhyming practice!

FIGURE IT OUT ANSWERS

Page 4: A rhyme is two or more words that sound alike.

Page 6: "Bat," "rat," "cat," and "pat" all belong to the "-at" family.

Page 8: "Humpty" and "Dumpty" rhyme. "Wall" and "fall" rhyme, too. They rhyme because they sound the same, and they're spelled the same except for the first letter.

Page 10: They rhyme because, in this case, "-un," "-on" and "-one" make the same sound.

Page 12: "Are" is the missing word. It rhymes with "star"!

Page 14: Rhythm is the flow of words in a sentence.

Page 16: "PRIN" is stressed and "ci" and "pal" are unstressed.

Page 18: The sentences can be rewritten as, "I LOVE to GO to SCHOOL. My FA-vorite CLASS is SCI-ence."

Page 20: Mouse: house, louse; **gate**: hate, rate, late; **boat**: goat, moat, wrote; **ran**: pan, can, man.

GLOSSARY

combine (kuhm-BYN) To arrange.

determine (dih-TURH-muhn) To cause something to happen in a certain way.

lyrics (LIHR-ihks) The words of a song.

poetry (POH-uh-tree) A kind of writing that often contains rhythm and rhymes.

pronounce (pruh-NOWNS) To say out loud.

stress (STREHS) The power given to a syllable or word to make it sound stronger than other syllables or words.

syllable (SIH-luh-buhl) A group of letters that make up part of a word and are pronounced together.

INDEX

WEBSITES

Due to the changing nature of Internet links, PowerKids Press has developed an online list of websites related to the subject of this book. This site is updated regularly. Please use this link to access the list: www.powerkidslinks.com/cls/rhym